GW01457987

BOOK ANALYSIS

Written by Jessica Wheeler

The Book Thief
BY MARKUS ZUSAK

MARKUS ZUSAK

AUSTRALIAN NOVELIST

- **Born in Sydney in 1975.**
- **Notable works:**
  - *The Messenger* (2002), novel
  - *Underdogs* (2011), anthology of Zusak's first three works
  - *Bridge of Clay* (2018), novel

Markus Zusak was born in Sydney, Australia to non-English-speaking parents. Zusak's mother was German and his father was Austrian. The stories they told Zusak and his three older siblings about their experiences of war-time in their home countries provided the inspiration for *The Book Thief.*

Zusak's passion for literature started at a young age, as did his aspiration to be an author. He started writing when he was 16, and eight years later his first book *Underdog* was published. This was the first book in a trilogy, from which the second and third instalments both won awards.

Zusak currently lives in New South Wales, Australia, with his wife Mika and his two children.

THE BOOK THIEF

WAR NOVEL NARRATED BY DEATH

- **Genre:** historical novel
- **Reference edition:** Zusak, M. (2012) *The Book Thief*. London: Definitions.
- **1st edition:** 2005
- **Themes:** humanity vs cruelty, courage, survival, poverty, books and the power of words, death, war, love

Zusak claimed in an interview that he intended this novel to be an exploration of the real-life experiences of German natives during the horrors of World War Two. The voice of Death narrates the story of a young girl who he calls 'the book thief'. Her name is Liesel Meminger and she has left an impression on the character of Death in the midst of the atrocities of the Nazi regime, and it is for this reason that Death tells her story.

Zusak's novel differs from many other stories that tell of experiences of life in Germany during the Second World War. He exposes the horrors of this time through a narrative that follows the life of a seemingly ordinary German girl, who in fact comes to represent an important lesson in morality, humanity and compassion by the end of the story. It is through the juxtaposition of childish innocence and heart-wrenching suffering that Zusak manages to deliver a compelling war narrative.

SUMMARY

A NEW HOME

Liesel travels by train with her mother and younger brother to the home of her new foster parents. Liesel's brother dies during the journey, and they must stop off to give him a funeral. The grave-digger's apprentice drops a book as he leaves the graveyard, and Liesel picks it up and keeps it as a memento of her brother. This marks the first stolen book that earns Liesel the name of 'book thief'. Liesel is then forced to say goodbye to her mother at the train station and is taken to the home of Hans and Rosa Hubermann – her foster parents. Liesel and Hans bond very quickly and establish a strong, loving relationship. Liesel has little memory of her real father and she appreciates Hans' kindness and care towards her; she therefore has no trouble calling Hans 'Papa'. Rosa brings Liesel with her to collect and deliver the laundry she does for the neighbours, and Liesel quickly progresses to doing the deliveries herself, making her more familiar with the other inhabitants of Molching.

Liesel starts school but is put into a class with the younger children because she cannot read. Hans finds out and begins teaching her the alphabet.

MAKING FRIENDS AND STEALING A SECOND BOOK

Liesel quickly becomes best friends with her neighbour Rudy Steiner. Rudy initially pesters her for a kiss, but Liesel refuses. A book burning is organised to celebrate Hitler's birthday. By this stage, Liesel has started to be able to read and has an appreciation for the value of books. The fact that the book burning is a form of censorship and the significance of the Nazi propaganda that goes along with it become clearer to Liesel. As a result, Liesel starts to harbour anti-Nazi sentiment, which her foster father warns her she must not express for fear of the consequences. As an act of rebellion, Liesel instead steals a book from the burning pile on the night of Hitler's birthday.

THE MAYOR'S WIFE

Liesel realises that Ilsa Hermann, the Mayor's wife, witnessed her stealing the book from the burning pile. Liesel initially avoids seeing her, but when they do come face to face Ilsa invites Liesel into her house and shows her the library full of books. In the meantime, the scene moves from Liesel in Molching to depict Max Vandenburg in his hiding place in Stuttgart. This foreshadows Max's entry into Liesel's life. Ilsa begins letting Liesel use the library to read. Liesel finds out that Ilsa had a son who died.

MAX ARRIVES

Max Vandenburg arrives at the Hubermanns' house seeking help and refuge. Hans tells Liesel the story of how Max's father saved his life in the First World War and that for this Hans vowed to protect and help his son if there was ever a need to. For the first few nights Max sleeps in the bedroom with Liesel, in the bed that was meant for her brother. Max then moves down to the basement and remains hidden. Life in the Hubermann household becomes centred around their shared secret – the Jew in the basement. Max falls ill from sleeping in the cold and damp basement. He and Liesel begin to bond as each has suffered loss and trauma in their short lives, and each is woken most nights by nightmares which stem from their experiences. Liesel turns 12, and as a belated birthday present Max makes her a book made from the pages of a copy of *Mein Kampf* given to him by Hans. The book tells the story of how Max and Liesel met, and how they became friends.

THE BOOK THIEF STRIKES AGAIN

The Mayor and his wife stop having their washing done by Rosa as the war progresses and everyone has to cut back. Liesel and Rudy later climb into the Mayor's house through an open window, and Liesel steals a book from the library.

TWO CLOSE CALLS

Max falls ill again and the Hubermanns fear that he may die. Liesel reads to him while he is unconscious and brings him small gifts. Eventually Max regains his health and returns once more to the basement. A short time later, Nazi Party members begin going from house to house to inspect the basements for a suitable bomb shelter. They check the Hubermanns' basement but luckily do not find Max.

AN ACT OF KINDNESS LEADS TO FEAR OF TROUBLE

The Jews who are being taken to Dachau concentration camp are paraded through Molching. Hans gives an old man who is struggling to walk with the other prisoners a piece of bread. Both are whipped in front of the crowd, and Hans fears that the Gestapo will come to his house to take him away and find Max there. As a result, Max leaves the Hubermanns' house. Hans is then conscripted into the German army and has to leave his family. There are further marches of Jews through Molching, and Liesel checks each to see if Max is amongst them. After another air raid, Rosa gives Liesel a gift that Max left for her – another book he made called 'The Word Shaker'. Hans is injured and sends a letter home to say that he will be returning briefly before going to Munich to take up a post doing office work. It is not long before Hans returns home to Molching.

A TRAGIC ENDING

Another group of Jews is marched through Liesel's village, and she sees that Max is amongst them. Bombs descend on the street where Liesel lives during the night. Everyone she knows and those she loves dearest are killed in the air raid. Liesel is spared as she was in the basement reading at the time of the bombing.

CHARACTER STUDY

LIESEL MEMINGER

Liesel is the main character in the novel. Death, the narrator, calls her 'the book thief' and the story reveals the reason for this. Liesel is introduced to the reader as a severely malnourished nine-year-old who has just experienced the loss of her six-year-old brother during the journey to their new foster parents' home. In this way, the character of Liesel is presented as one who has suffered greatly from a young age. Her sufferings seem to build her character into one of strength and spirit. Liesel is also compassionate and cares deeply about those around her. These traits combine to form a character who is courageous in the face of injustice and suffering. She cannot stand by and accept the atrocities that happen around her; instead, she is led by her sense of morality and what is right even though she is a child. As Liesel matures, she continues to display these initial characteristics, as well as an increasing ability to think and decide for herself what to make of the events and people she encounters. Liesel Meminger is not only the protagonist of this novel; she is the heroine of her own story.

HANS HUBERMANN

Hans is Liesel's foster father and husband to Rosa Hubermann. His inherent kindness is clear from the moment Hans enters the story and is able to coax Liesel from the car into her new home for the first time. A loving relationship is established very quickly between Liesel and Hans as he supports her through the trauma of losing her brother, being separated from her mother and having to start her life over. The fatherly love and kindness that Hans shows to Liesel is a foundational component of his character. Hans shares some traits with Liesel; for example, he is a free thinker who is critical of the Nazi regime, he is compassionate and he is courageous. It is Hans who teaches Liesel to read.

ROSA HUBERMANN

Rosa is Liesel's foster mother, and wife to Hans. When Rosa enters the story, she is portrayed as harsh and mean. She does not seem to empathise with Liesel over the traumatic experience that she is going through. Her abusive language is regular, with words like "saumensch", "saukerl" and "arschloch" heading her vocabulary. The narrator provides some facts about Rosa, citing that she "possessed the unique ability to aggravate almost anyone she ever met. But she *did* love Liesel Meminger. Her way of showing it just happened to be strange. It involved bashing her with wooden spoon and words, at various intervals." (p. 35). Rosa spends most of her time verbally abusing Hans and complaining that he is no good to her as a husband and that is why she has to supplement their income by washing clothes for the wealthier inhabitants of their village. Despite the impression this gives, Rosa loves her husband and Liesel very much and works hard to look after them. When Hans is sent away, Rosa misses him terribly and hugs his accordion at night as it is a reminder of him. A softer side of Rosa is shown when Max Vandenburg arrives in the story, as Rosa immediately worries and cares for him. Rosa does not hesitate to take Max in and protect him, despite the serious danger it puts her and her family in.

MAX VANDENBURG

Max is the son of a friend of Hans Hubermann's, and the man who saved his life in the First World War. He is a Jew and is therefore in need of refuge from the Nazi Party. Max suffers a lot of guilt as a result of leaving his family and putting the Hubermanns in danger by hiding in their home. Max used to fist fight when he was a child, and this fighting spirit remains with him throughout the duration of the story. Max shows a resilience and determination to survive, thereby mirroring some characteristics that Liesel also displays. Both Max and Liesel are haunted by their experiences of suffering in the form of nightmares. Furthermore, both characters share a genuine kindness and affection toward each other.

ANALYSIS

DEATH AS NARRATOR

Zusak's choice of narrator is an interesting and unique one. The story is told by a voice which represents the personification of death. The character traditionally associated with the event of death is the Grim Reaper. However, the narrator in this story never identifies themselves by a name. Instead, the reader comes to know who the voice of the narrator belongs to slowly over the first pages of the book as the narrator describes how he/she comes at the moment death occurs to take a person's soul away. As such, the narrative establishes a style which often implicitly delivers details and knowledge to the reader.

Having Death as the narrator of this story evokes the sense that the tale is being told from the perspective of a being who sees all. The narrative voice therefore seems to come from a place that no human being could occupy, and this lends a sense of importance to the narrative perspective. The reader automatically trusts in the reliability of the narrator. The voice of Death reinforces this belief through the use of foreshadowing and by giving the reader clues as to what will happen in the story. In this way, an expectation is repeatedly set up in the reader which is fulfilled and, consequently, the confidence the reader has in Death as a narrator is strengthened.

Death exhibits a compassionate nature throughout the novel, which is potentially inconsistent with expectations of this character. Dying is something that many people fear, and portrayals of the Grim Reaper character are rarely friendly. However, Zusak has personified Death in such a way that he/she sees beyond the souls that they are tasked with collecting to the lives that these souls have lived and the world that has encapsulated their experiences. Zusak gives his narrator a heart and, arguably, a soul of their own. He has constructed a character who is representative of Death, but who cares – about the souls he/she arrives to collect, and more importantly, the ones who remain for a while longer before it is their time. It is this element of humanity and compassion that ultimately leads Death to tell the story of Liesel Meminger, and that also gives *The Book*

Thief a distinctive, unique and breathtakingly powerful narrative voice.

BOOKS AND THE POWER OF WORDS

When Liesel is introduced to the reader, she is a poverty-stricken nine-year-old girl who does not even possess the ability to read. She suffers the further losses of her brother and mother, and these are marked by the first book that comes into her possession. This book is called *The Gravedigger's Handbook;* however, it is not the content of this book that is of utmost importance, but what it represents – a new beginning. The narrator explains that Liesel took the book from the snow when the gravedigger's apprentice dropped it, because she wanted to have a reminder of the last time she was with her brother. Soon after this, Liesel has to say goodbye to her mother and her life changes forever.

Hans begins to teach Liesel how to read, despite the fact that he is far from a literary scholar himself. *The Gravedigger's Handbook* is the first book that Hans and Liesel read together. Again, it is not the content of the book or the meaning of the words that is significant, but the words themselves, and the fact that they constitute something shared. This theme also carries into Liesel's relationship with Ilsa Hermann. The library becomes a place where these two characters share the story of their losses with each other. Amongst the words that are contained in the many books on the shelves, a bond is created between the wealthy Mayor's wife and the poor, hungry washwoman's daughter. Liesel's love and appreciation for books grows in this library, which provides her with her next literary treasure.

Books and words alone make up only half of the central theme of this story. Liesel is christened by the narrator with the name of 'the book thief', and it is the act of stealing the books that makes the power of words in the midst of the horrors of Nazi Germany even more compelling. Ilsa tries to gift a book to Liesel, but she refuses to accept it and chooses to steal the book instead. It is through the act of thievery that Liesel seems to truly claim back the words, and their potential to enact change.

The Nazi Party was clearly aware of this power, as is demonstrated by the ceremonious act of burning all the books that could be found by non-Aryan authors. Liesel's daring and rebellious act of stealing a book from the burning pile is potentially the most symbolic in the novel. It is this simple and spontaneous decision which represents a child's pure resistance to the grotesque control exhibited by Nazi ideology.

Another symbolic action which relates to the power of books and words is carried out by Max Vandenburg. Max paints over the pages of Adolf Hitler's *Mein Kampf* in order to create a blank canvas upon which to write the story of how he and Liesel met and became friends. In using the pages of the book written by the man who is responsible for his oppression and suffering, Max undermines the power of Hitler's words with his own. The words which have inflicted pain and horror upon so many are replaced by ones which depict kindness, love and friendship.

By the end of the novel, Ilsa again provides Liesel with the tool and inspiration to employ words to combat the hatred and despair that she feels living in Nazi Germany. Ilsa gives Liesel a book in which she writes her own story – the story which Death feels called upon to tell. This is a testament to the fact that words have such power, that they can even leave a lasting impression on the soul of Death.

NAZI GERMANY

Zusak's novel is set against the backdrop of World War Two, during which Adolf Hitler and the Nazi Party were responsible for devastating atrocities against the German nation, and beyond. Zusak has chosen to foreground the everyday lived experiences of a young German girl; a choice that contrasts with many other novels written in or about this era, which often take as their direct focus the victimisation of the Jewish population. This is not to say that Zusak overlooks the ordeals and sufferings felt by so many at the hands of Hitler and the Nazi Party, but instead he has chosen to frame them in a new way.

Through the use of Death as narrator, and by positioning Liesel as the main character of the novel, the reader experiences the horrors of this time differently to such texts as *The Diary of Anne Frank, Man's Search for Meaning*, or even *Schindler's List* – three prominent Holocaust texts.

FURTHER REFLECTION

SOME QUESTIONS TO THINK ABOUT...

- Would you say that this is a Holocaust novel? Explain your answer.
- What is the effect of having the character of Death narrate the story? Imagine the story of Liesel's life was told from her own perspective. How would the story be framed differently?
- Do you think the title of the novel is fitting? Would you have chosen a different title for the book?
- Comment on Zusak's use of the senses in the novel, and the way that he intertwines and confuses them in his descriptions.
- In the final line of the book, Death tells the reader "I am haunted by humans". Why is this?
- If you could ask one character in the story a question, what would it be?
- Do you see the narrator as male or female? Why?

- Zusak uses foreshadowing in his novel. Consider the effect this has on the pace and delivery of the story.
- Compare *The Book Thief* to one other novel you have read that is set during the time of the Second World War. How are they similar? How do they differ? Do they send the same message or evoke the same emotions in you as a reader?

We want to hear from you!
Leave a comment on your online library
and share your favourite books on social media!

FURTHER READING

REFERENCE EDITION

- Zusak, M. (2012) *The Book Thief.* London: Definitions.

ADDITIONAL SOURCES

- Hudson, C. (2010) Interview with Markus Zusak, Author of The Book Thief and I Am the Messenger. *Mother Daughter Book Club.* [Online]. [Accessed 14 December 2018]. Available from: <https://motherdaughterbookclub.com/2010/02/interview-with-markus-zusak-author-of-the-book-thief-and-i-am-the-messenger/>

ADAPTATIONS

- *The Book Thief.* (2013) [Film]. Brian Percival. Dir. USA: Fox 2000 Pictures, Sunswept Entertainment, Studio Babelsberg, TSG Entertainment.

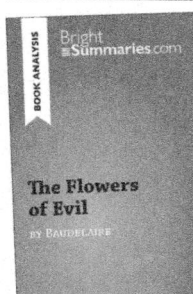

www.brightsummaries.com

Ebook EAN: 9782808016476

Paperback EAN: 9782808016483

Legal Deposit: D/2018/12603/584

Cover: © Primento

Digital conception by Primento, the digital partner of
publishers.

Printed in Great Britain
by Amazon